I0820915

The FLORIDA KEYS

by Pam Berkman

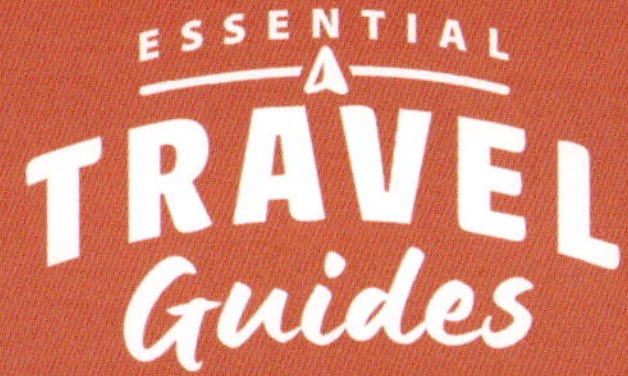

Essential Library
An Imprint of Abdo Publishing
abdobooks.com

ABDOBOOKS.COM

Published by Abdo Publishing, a division of ABDO, PO Box 398166, Minneapolis, Minnesota 55439.

Printed in China.
052025
092025

Cover Photo: Shutterstock Images
Interior Photos: iStockphoto, 4–5; Brian Parker/Alamy, 9; V. R. Mrochek/Nature and People, 12; William C. Bunce/Shutterstock Images, 16–17; Reinhard Dirscherl/ullstein bild/Getty Images, 20; Brett Seymour/US National Park Service, 23, 76–77; Jeff Greenberg/Universal Images Group/Getty Images, 24–25; Stephen Frink/The Image Bank/Getty Images, 29, 71, 78–79; Peter Titmuss/Alamy, 30; Buddy Mays/Corbis Historical/Getty Images, 33; ThePalmer/E+/Getty Images, 34–35; Stephen Saks Photography/Alamy, 38; Felix Mizioznikov/Shutterstock Images, 41, 51; Kemter/E+/Getty Images, 44–45; John A. Anderson/Shutterstock Images, 48; Simon Dannhauer/Shutterstock Images, 52–53; Tom Salyer/Alamy, 55; Shutterstock Images, 56, 60–61, 64, 72, 85, 98; Diann C. Johnson/Moment/Getty Images, 59; Kathy Willens/AP Images, 67; Jeffrey Greenberg/Universal Images Group/Getty Images, 69; Craig Hinton/Shutterstock Images, 74; Barry Mansell/Nature Picture Library, 82; Gregory Sweeney/Moment/Getty Images, 86, 89; Cavan Images/Getty Images, 90–91; Paul Franklin/Alamy, 93; Red Line Editorial, 101 (United States), 101 (Florida Keys)

Editor: Christa Kelly
Series Designer: Joshua Olson

Library of Congress Control Number: 2024948596

PUBLISHER'S CATALOGING-IN-PUBLICATION DATA

Names: Berkman, Pam, author.
Title: The Florida keys / by Pam Berkman
Description: Minneapolis, Minnesota: Abdo Publishing, 2026 | Series: Essential travel guides | Includes online resources and index.
Identifiers: ISBN 9781098297084 (lib. bdg.) | ISBN 9798384919605 (ebook)
Subjects: LCSH: Florida Keys (Fla.)--Juvenile literature. | Travel--Juvenile literature. | United States--Guidebooks--Juvenile literature. | Florida, South--Juvenile literature. | Historic sites--Juvenile literature.
Classification: DDC 917.594--dc23

CONTENTS

CHAPTER ONE
THE ISLAND CHAIN 4

CHAPTER TWO
THE NORTHERNMOST KEYS 16

CHAPTER THREE
KEY LARGO 24

CHAPTER FOUR
ISLAMORADA 34

CHAPTER FIVE
THE MIDDLE KEYS 44

CHAPTER SIX
THE LOWER KEYS 52

CHAPTER SEVEN
KEY WEST AND DRY TORTUGAS NATIONAL PARK 60

CHAPTER EIGHT
ANIMALS OF THE KEYS 78

CHAPTER NINE
SPORTS IN THE KEYS 90

ESSENTIAL FACTS 100
GLOSSARY 102
ADDITIONAL RESOURCES 104
SOURCE NOTES 106
INDEX 110
ABOUT THE AUTHOR 112

CHAPTER ONE

THE ISLAND CHAIN

At the southernmost edge of the United States, trailing off the edge of Florida like a string of beads, lie the Florida Keys. These coral, limestone, and sandbar islands formed 125,000 years ago. About 100,000 years ago, when sea levels dropped during the last ice age, these once-underwater coral reefs and sandbars were revealed. They formed an archipelago—a scattered group of islands in a body of water.

Gradually, ocean currents deposited sediments that built up on the surface of the coral reefs, making the Keys a coral cay archipelago. Approximately 15,000 years ago, the ice melted and water levels rose, flooding the area and bringing more

More than 1,700 islands make up the Florida Keys.

geographical changes. This left the Keys with a wide variety of interdependent habitats.

The Florida Keys extend about 220 miles (350 km), stretching from Virginia Key in the north to Key West in the south.[1] Key West is not only the southernmost key but also the southernmost point in the continental United States, sitting just 90 miles (145 km) north of Cuba.[2] Today, the Keys' unique environment attracts tourists, scientists, and historians.

> **It's the best place I've ever been any time, anywhere.[3]**
> ***—Author Ernest Hemingway on Key West***

The Prehistoric Keys

The first humans in the Florida Keys were nomadic groups following large animals for food. Mastodons, extinct elephant-like mammals, roamed the area 14,000 years ago alongside camels, mammoths, bison, and horses. Though these animals became extinct in the Keys, the islands remained abundant with smaller mammals, shellfish, and other wildlife. Pottery evidence exists of a prehistoric culture, now known as the Glades Culture, that stretched from the Keys to northern Miami as early as 500 BCE. American Indian groups, including the Calusa and Tequesta nations, were hunting and harvesting other resources in the Keys by about 800 CE. Ancient artifacts from this era have been discovered at Crane Point Hammock near the modern city of Marathon in the Keys.

The Florida Keys were a perfect location for these nations. Resources were plentiful, offering everything the people needed. They ate lobsters, fish, turtles, deer, and raccoons, supplemented by fruits such as sea grapes and cocoplums. They made tools and weapons from conch shells and sharks' teeth.

In 1513, Spanish explorer Juan Ponce de León became the first European to reach the area. He landed in Florida and charted the Keys. Looking at the map, he thought the islands looked like men in distress, so he called them Los Martires, or "the Martyrs," but the name didn't stick. The region instead became known as the Keys after the Spanish word for a small island, *cayo*.

European Powers and the Seminoles

Tensions between settlers and native nations rose as Europeans began to move into the Keys. Spanish settlers began arriving in Florida in 1565. As the European powers struggled among one another to gain control of North American lands, the area changed hands several times. It was first controlled by the Spanish until 1763 and then by the British from 1763 to 1783. During the period of British control, large numbers of enslaved people were brought to Florida. The two British colonies there at the time of the Revolutionary War (1775–1783) were East Florida and West Florida. The colonies sided with the British.

Spain took control of the area again in 1783 after the Revolutionary War. After the War of 1812 (1812–1815), US forces occupied and attacked parts of Spanish Florida. Spain ceded control of the colony to the United States in 1821, and Florida became a territory of the United States. It was admitted as a US state in 1845.

In the 1700s, members of the Creek Nation in nearby Georgia and Alabama, along with members of other nations such as the Yuchi and Yamasee, had begun to migrate to the Keys. Escaped enslaved Africans also fled to the region. At the time, the Spanish encouraged enslaved Africans to escape the British colonies and flee to Florida, where they were offered freedom in exchange for converting to Catholicism. American Indians and former enslaved Africans intermarried and became known as the Seminoles.

By 1800, violence was escalating between European settlers and the Seminoles. The US government fought three wars with the Seminole Nation between 1817 and

1858, causing many settlers to leave the Upper and Middle Keys. Seminole leader Osceola was captured in 1837 after being lured to a supposed truce, and the US government forced most of the Seminoles to relocate west of the Mississippi River. Only 200 to 300 Seminole people remained in Florida. The Seminole population slowly rose, and today, about 3,000 Seminole people live in the state.[4]

Wrecking

Wrecking is the trade of salvaging shipwrecks and selling the goods for profit. In 1822, the first permanent European settlers began to arrive in the Keys. Wrecking was an important industry for these people.

Today, a statue in Key West honors Florida's wreckers.

The Gulf Stream, a powerful ocean current in the North Atlantic that begins in the Gulf of Mexico, passes near the Florida Keys. Though it provided an ideal shipping route to Mexico and the Caribbean, the chain of reefs and shallow channels made shipwrecks common. Raiding these unlucky ships for materials and goods became a staple business and way of life for European settlers.

As the volume of shipping increased, so did the wrecking. By the 1800s, a wrecked ship was being salvaged off the Keys almost once a week. From about 1850 to 1900, Key West was the largest, richest city in the entire state, partly due to the wrecking trade. The city also profited greatly from harvesting undersea sponges.

A major center for wrecking was a small but prosperous settlement on Indian Key. In 1840, Indian Key was attacked by a group of American Indians who killed settlers and burned buildings to the ground. Today, travelers can visit the ruins of this ghost town in Indian Key Historic State Park.

The increasing construction of lighthouses along the Keys' shores and the use of steamships, which could be steered regardless of wind conditions, reduced the frequency of shipwrecks and ended the wrecking trade. Today, visitors can explore several shipwrecks up close on the Shipwreck Trail in the Florida Keys National Marine Sanctuary, on the Maritime Heritage Trail in Biscayne National Park, and in Dry Tortugas National Park.

The Overseas Railroad

For decades, the Keys were an isolated part of Florida. This changed when businessman Henry Flagler designed the Overseas Railroad. Seeing the potential for a railway route to the Keys, Flagler worked with engineer James Meredith to build the 128-mile (206 km) Key West Extension.[5] Traversing islands and open water, this railroad was sometimes called the Eighth Wonder of the World.

The railroad was completed in 1912, despite the three hurricanes that swept through the Keys while the railway was being built. Construction took seven years and cost more than $50 million, about $1.62 billion in today's money.[6] The railroad opened

Hurricanes and the Florida Keys

Hurricanes have shaped much of the history of the Florida Keys. The 1935 Labor Day Hurricane is considered the strongest hurricane ever to hit the United States. It killed more than 400 people. The 1622 hurricane wrecked several Spanish treasure ships, some of which are still submerged in Dry Tortugas National Park. The Great Havana Hurricane washed away Sand Key in 1846. The island later reappeared in a new location. In 2017, Hurricane Irma caused $50 billion in damages, making it Florida's most expensive storm at the time.[7]

the Keys to visitors and gave farmers a fast way to get their products to major cities. The railroad ran for more than 20 years before being damaged in the fierce 1935 Labor Day Hurricane. It was replaced by the Overseas Highway.

Completed in 1938 and still the main route through the Florida Keys, the Overseas Highway reconnected the islands. The 113-mile (182 km) road was built as one of the public works projects that employed workers during the Great Depression. One of the world's longest overwater roads, it features 42 bridges. One, known as the Seven Mile Bridge, spans almost seven miles

At any time during construction, more than 4,000 workers were employed building the Overseas Railroad.

(11 km).[8] Travelers along the highway can gaze out at the beautiful ocean beyond, stretching out into the distance.

Parks and Sanctuaries

Today, visitors flock to the Florida Keys to experience the Caribbean climate and the relaxed, friendly culture of the islands. Rare wildlife also draws ecotourists. The primary industries in the Keys are fishing, scuba diving, and tourism.

The Florida Keys teem with a vast tapestry of plant and animal life. The Keys are home to animals that cannot be found anywhere else, such as the tiny Key deer. Coral reefs provide homes for more than 600 species of fish.[9] Sea turtles and endangered manatees swim in the waters.

The Florida Keys contain two national parks. The parks, Biscayne National Park and Dry Tortugas National Park, are both almost entirely underwater. The Keys also boast four national wildlife refuges and ten state parks, including John Pennekamp Coral Reef State Park, the first undersea park in the United States.

Many other spectacular parks, reserves, and sanctuaries are located in the Keys, such as the Florida Keys National Marine Sanctuary, where more than 6,000 species of animals thrive.[10] This sanctuary includes almost all the waters around the Keys. Most of the underwater parks in the Keys fall within the sanctuary's boundaries. Established in 1990, the sanctuary covers 3,600 square miles (9,300 sq km) and stretches from Biscayne National Park to Dry Tortugas National Park.[11] It also encompasses about 150 miles (240 km) of the Florida Reef, home to 45 species of hard corals.[12]

Under the waves of the Florida Keys National Marine Sanctuary lies a trail of nine shipwrecks. The shipwrecks stretch along the length of the Keys, from the remains of the *City of Washington* east of Key Largo to the wreck of the *Amesbury* west of Key West. The *Benwood, Duane, Eagle, San Pedro, Adelaide Baker, Thunderbolt*, and *North America* lie between them. The ships date from the 1700s to the 1980s, representing various eras in the seafaring history of the Florida Keys.

Coral Nurseries

Climate change is causing ocean temperatures to rise, killing fragile coral ecosystems. Between 1984 and 2024, the volume of healthy coral in the Florida Keys decreased by more than 90 percent.[13] Conservationists battle this trend by growing corals in special underwater nurseries to repopulate the damaged reefs. These nurseries help nurture small corals until they can be moved and placed on existing reefs. There are more than a dozen coral nurseries in the Florida Keys, carefully situated close to the reefs that the young corals will help restore.

The Overseas Highway is the main way to travel across the Keys. While on a key, tourists can walk, bike, and bus around the island. Businesses provide ferries, kayaks, and paddleboards to get travelers to areas accessible only by water. Hotels are plentiful in popular towns, and camping is available on many of the islands. Winter is the peak travel season because the weather is dry, sunny, and temperate.

Each key is unique. Some, such as No Name Key, are home to quiet sanctuaries for rare species. Others, such as Key Largo and Key West, contain bustling cities. Whether visitors are looking for sailing, fishing, wildlife, or historic towns and museums, they will find something fascinating in the Florida Keys.

Everglades National Park

Adjacent to the Florida Keys area lies Everglades National Park. The park was established in 1947 after an almost 20-year effort by Ernest Coe and Marjory Stoneman Douglas. Their goal was to protect the Everglades, an enormous wetland wilderness, from dredging and draining damage. In 2000, a 30-year plan to restore the natural water flow to the Everglades went into action. Today, the park provides homes for many endangered and threatened species, including the manatee, the American crocodile, and the elusive Florida panther.

CHAPTER
TWO

THE NORTHERNMOST KEYS

When people refer to the Florida Keys, most mean the string of keys from Key Largo to Key West. However, several islands are located farther north. These islands are known as the Northernmost Keys.

The Northernmost Keys are made of more than 40 islands, all accessible only by boat. To the far north is a group of islands called the Ragged Keys. At least one of these islands used to be inhabited. South of these islands is Boca Chita Key, followed by Sands Key. Farther south is a long, thin island called Elliott Key. To the south are Totten Key and Old Rhodes Key. Smaller keys are scattered across the region.

The Northernmost Keys are not connected to the rest of the keys by the Overseas Highway.

Biscayne National Park

Many of the islands that make up the Northernmost Keys are part of Biscayne National Park. The largest of the islands in the park is Elliott Key. The island was once home to settlers who farmed pineapples and engaged in wrecking and sponging. The key is known for the dense forests along its coastline. The forests are filled with mangrove trees, tropical trees that grow in salty swamps.

Boca Chita Key is the most visited island in Biscayne National Park. Visitors can hike the island's half-mile (0.8 km) trail to see the key's beauty. The hike gives visitors a stunning view of the island's 65-foot (20 m) ornamental lighthouse.[1] Both Elliott Key and Boca Chita Key have facilities for picnicking and camping. Campsites on Elliott Key and Boca Chita Key are simple, and some visitors

The Spite Highway

During the 1950s, land developers became keenly interested in the Northernmost Keys, which were undeveloped and not connected to the rest of the archipelago by the Overseas Railroad. The developers proposed plans to build a city, an industrial seaport, and an airport on the keys. A group of locals resisted, arguing that the area should be designated a national park instead. The battle was bitter, with developers eventually building the so-called Spite Highway across Elliott Key. In 1968, a bill creating Biscayne National Park was signed into law by President Lyndon B. Johnson, and the highway was converted into a hiking trail.

report being plagued by no-see-ums, tiny bugs whose bites pack a big itch.

Between the adjacent islands of Totten Key and Old Rhodes Key is Jones Lagoon. The lagoon is surrounded by a cluster of small islands. Its waterways are rich with opportunities for snorkeling, kayaking, and canoeing.

Sections of Biscayne Bay and the Atlantic Ocean waters surrounding these keys are part of Biscayne National Park too, leaving 95 percent of the 270-square-mile (700 sq km) park underwater.[2] Part of the Florida Reef, the world's third-largest reef, lies within the park. The reef is home to more than 500 species of fish, including parrotfish, angelfish, wrasses, and butterfly fish.[3] The reef also hosts sea cucumbers and Christmas tree worms.

Biscayne National Park also extends onto Florida's mainland. This is where visitors can find the Biscayne

Christmas Tree Worms

Christmas tree worms inhabit coral reefs all over the world, including the reefs in the Florida Keys. These worms are about 1.5 inches (3.8 cm) long and come in a variety of colors.[4] Each worm has two stalks. These stalks are called crowns and are made of hairlike appendages called radioles. The worms use their crowns to breathe and eat. Each radiole collects microscopic floating plants for the worms to digest. The crowns have several tiers, making the stalks reminiscent of pine trees and earning the worms their festive name.

Christmas tree worms come in a variety of stunning colors.

National Park Institute. The institute can assist visitors with setting up trips to different keys. It offers boat trips, as well as paddling, snorkeling, and scuba-diving expeditions. People are advised to make advance reservations. Visitors who take a snorkeling or scuba-diving trip can explore the underwater sections of the park. These activities allow visitors to glimpse some of the park's marine wildlife and explore the six shipwrecks that sit on the park's seafloor.

> "The water of Biscayne Bay is exceedingly clear. In no part can one fail to clearly distinguish objects on the bottom.[5]"
>
> *—Biologist Hugh Smith*

Guests with their own boats can navigate to the Northernmost

Keys themselves. Before heading off the mainland, they can check the tidal charts at Dante Fascell Visitor Center. The visitor center's location on Convoy Point, a section of land jutting into Biscayne Bay, also makes it an ideal place to launch kayaks and canoes.

Cleaning Up the Park

Visitors who want to make a meaningful contribution to preserving the ecosystem of the Florida Keys have a unique opportunity. The Biscayne National Park Institute offers marine debris cleanup trips. Volunteers can spend a day paddling a kayak and collecting litter, cleaning the shoreline, or removing fishing debris from fishing sites. This work helps conserve the Keys' sensitive habitats and protect the region's marine wildlife. Interested travelers can contact the Biscayne National Park Institute for more information.

The Maritime Heritage Trail

One of Biscayne National Park's most popular features is its undersea Maritime Heritage Trail. At least six historic sunken ships rest within Biscayne National Park on this watery pathway. The shipwrecks date from 1966 to as far back as the 1700s. The trail can be followed only by boat. Those who set off along the trail can explore the ruined ships and aquatic life under the park's surface.

Some of the shipwrecks along the Maritime Heritage Trail are accessible to snorkelers. One such wreck is the *Arratoon Apcar*. The remains of the ship lie only a few hundred yards from the Fowey Rocks Lighthouse, where the ship ran aground in 1878. Also accessible to snorkelers is the *Mandalay*. Outfitted in mahogany, brass, and ivory,

The *Mandalay* was being used as a cruise ship when it sank. None of its passengers were seriously injured during the wreck.

this steel-hulled schooner sank in 1966. Its skeletal remains are embedded on Long Reef. The final wreck snorkelers can explore is a nameless wooden ship. Dating back to the 1800s, this site is known today as the Schooner Wreck.

Other wrecks along the Maritime Heritage Trail can be explored only by scuba divers. One such wreck is the *Erl King*. This massive iron-hulled steamer sank in 1891. Like the *Mandalay*, the *Erl King* ran aground on Long Reef. Today, it sits on the reef under more than 18 feet (5 m) of water.[6]

Another wreck that can be explored only by scuba divers is the *Alicia*. This ship was carrying precious items including silk and silverware when it was wrecked in a 1905 storm. US salvage laws were rewritten in response to a fight over the lost goods that involved 70 groups of wreckers. The final shipwreck along the Maritime Heritage Trail is the *Lugano*. The ship sank in 1913 and now lies beneath 25 feet (8 m) of water on Long Reef.[7]

The Fowey Rocks Lighthouse is an iconic stop on the Maritime Heritage Trail. Also known as the Eye of Miami, the lighthouse was completed in 1878. A century and a half of hurricanes have raged around this lighthouse. Though the lighthouse is closed to the public, visitors can snorkel around the historic building's base.

CHAPTER THREE

KEY LARGO

Stretching 30 miles (50 km) from tip to tip, Key Largo is the largest island in the Florida Keys.[1] The island lies between the Everglades and Florida Bay to the west and the Atlantic Ocean to the east. Key Largo boasts the greatest concentration of dive sites in the Keys, plus prime opportunities for snorkeling, fishing, and camping.

Northern Key Largo is home to Dagny Johnson Key Largo Hammock Botanical State Park. Founded in 1982, the park covers more than 2,400 acres (1,000 ha).[2] This massive park is home to a wide range of wildlife, making it a popular spot for tourists. Eighty-four protected species make their homes in the park, including animals such as the Key Largo woodrat and

More than 12,000 people live on Key Largo.

the American crocodile and plants such as wild cotton and mahogany mistletoe.[3]

Some visitors come to see the park's magnificent butterflies. Those who are lucky may see Julia butterflies, zebra longwings, and giant swallowtails flying overhead. Birders keep watch for herons and birds of prey. Paleontologists look for coral fossils embedded in the park's rock walls.

The park is also a popular destination for bikers and hikers. There are more than six miles (10 km) of trails, most of which are paved and accessible for both bicycles and wheelchairs.[4] Photographers can find spots along the trails to stop and capture the park's natural beauty.

Key Limes

Key Largo was once known for its Key lime plantations. Key limes are smaller than Persian limes, with a delicate, thin skin and noticeably fragrant smell. The limes' juice is one of the main ingredients in Key lime pie. Though often associated with the Florida Keys, this fruit originally came from Southeast Asia. Many Key lime plantations were devastated by the Great Miami Hurricane of 1926. After the storm, most US lime farms switched to growing the hardier Persian limes.

John Pennekamp Coral Reef State Park

The jewel in Key Largo's crown of natural wonders is John Pennekamp Coral Reef State Park, the first undersea park in the United States. The park forms a strip 25 miles (40 km) long and three miles (5 km) wide off the key's east coast.[5] It protects part of the only living coral reef in the continental United States.

John Pennekamp Coral Reef State Park was established in 1963. It was named after conservationist John Pennekamp. Today, it's a gorgeous park full of adventure and opportunity. In this watery wonderland, visitors can snorkel among schools of tropical fish, scuba dive to an undersea sculpture, and kayak among mangrove trees.

> **One [of the most exciting moments of my career] would be when I first dived on a coral reef and I was able to move among a world of unrevealed complexity.[6]**
>
> ***—Naturalist David Attenborough***

At night, visitors can camp in the park. The park has facilities to accommodate tents and recreational vehicles, but sites can fill up as much as 11 months in advance, so reservations are recommended. Visitors can also stay overnight in their private boats.

In the late fall and winter, campers are invited to nightly park activities at the Point, a central event spot at the campground's entrance. The Point has benches, an outdoor screen, and a fire circle. Nightly events include ranger talks and crafts. Visitors can stop at the ranger station for a pass and a program schedule.

Ocean Activities

One magical way to see John Pennekamp Coral Reef State Park is to take a tour in a glass-bottom boat. Park visitors can book a ride on the *Spirit of Pennekamp*, a 65-foot (20 m) catamaran with a glass bottom.[7] The boat takes visitors on a two-and-a-half-hour tour of the magnificent Molasses Reef. There, guests can gaze through the boat's floor to see the underwater world below. Visitors can search for the more than 600 species of fish and 70 species of corals that live in the park's waters.[8] Fortunate guests may even spot a barracuda or sea turtle.

Snorkeling and scuba diving are other ways for visitors to immerse themselves in the park. Park rangers offer guided trips. Snorkel boat trips run four times a day, offering a two-and-a-half-hour adventure. The trip includes 90 minutes of reef exploration, allowing guests to observe the park's vibrant corals and marine life up close.

The most famous snorkeling destination at the park is the underwater *Christ of the Abyss* sculpture, which is located six miles (10 km) offshore. This 8.5-foot (2.6 m) bronze statue is a copy of a similar sculpture off the coast

The *Christ of the Abyss* statue is a copy of an Italian sculpture. The original statue was created and submerged to honor a deceased scuba diver.

Don't Miss It!

The Cannon Beach Shipwreck

A sunken ship was carefully assembled off the shore of Cannon Beach to give beachgoers an authentic sense of a shipwreck. The wreck is close to shore. This allows casual swimmers and snorkelers to explore a wreck without needing scuba training.

Artifacts from real Spanish shipwrecks were arranged to make the sunken ship feel realistic. Among the items on the seafloor are submerged cannons pointing out from the ship as if they were defending the boat against an enemy fleet. These cannons were originally from a ship in the 1715 Spanish Fleet, which was wrecked in a hurricane off the east coast of Florida.

At the northeast end of the shipwreck is an anchor. The anchor belonged to a vessel in the 1733 Spanish Fleet that was destroyed in a hurricane. A buoy marks the location of the anchor.

of Portofino Peninsula in northern Italy.[9] Corals have grown on the surface of the sculpture.

The Florida Keys' Corals

Many types of corals live off the coast of the Florida Keys. Lettuce corals are leaflike. Staghorn corals look like masses of tangled antlers. Elkhorn corals look similar but have a more flattened shape. Purple sea fan corals resemble lacy fans, while green sea fan corals are yellow-green and smaller. Shrimp and small invertebrate animals hide among finger corals. Brain corals grow in large, rounded lumps and are lined with grooves. Sea plume corals resemble stringy feathers. Fire corals are usually beige with a green tint. Those who touch them receive a burning sting.

Visitors looking to explore the park from the water's surface can try kayaking, canoeing, or paddleboarding. After renting equipment from the visitor center, tourists can explore the area along the park's aquatic trails. Kayakers, paddleboarders, and canoers can take a journey through the park's mangrove forests. The trees' roots provide homes for sponges, mangrove oysters, tunicates, and algae. More animals live near the trees. Passersby may spy crabs, shrimp, juvenile lobsters, fish, and seahorses zipping in and out of the mangrove's root structures. Lucky visitors may even spot a manatee.

There are two human-created beaches at John Pennekamp Coral Reef State Park. Cannon Beach is a popular spot for snorkeling. Just 100 feet (30 m) away from the shore is a staged shipwreck.[10] The wreck is easily accessible to snorkelers. Snorkelers can also admire the reef fish and other aquatic wildlife that live in the area's seagrass. Far Beach is dotted with palm trees. Visitors can relax under a tree, stretch out in the sun, or take a soothing swim. The beach is also wheelchair accessible.

Florida Keys Wild Bird Center

Farther south down Key Largo is the Florida Keys Wild Bird Center in Tavernier. The rehabilitation center was founded in 1991 by Laura Quinn. Quinn was a math teacher. After Quinn and her husband moved to the Florida Keys, she became interested in the area's native birds. She worked with veterinarian Robert Foley to learn to care for wounded and orphaned birds. Quinn's dedication and love of birds earned her the nickname Bird Lady.

Today, the sanctuary rehabilitates injured birds and releases them back into the wild. The center also cares for

Mangroves

Mangroves are specially adapted trees and shrubs that grow in tropical and subtropical areas. They grow in low-oxygen soil, where slow-moving waters allow fine sediments to accumulate. There are 80 species of mangroves worldwide. Three of these species are common in the Florida Keys.[11] Tourists can find red mangrove, black mangrove, and white mangrove trees across the string of islands.

birds that are unable to return to the wild. Tourists can visit the sanctuary and learn about its work. They can also see more than 60 birds from nearly 30 species.[12]

After decades of caring for wild birds, Laura Quinn passed away in 2010.

CHAPTER FOUR

ISLAMORADA

Islamorada, often called the Village of Islands, is a collection of six islands in the Upper Keys. These islands are Plantation Key, Windley Key, Upper Matecumbe Key, Lower Matecumbe Key, Indian Key, and Lignumvitae Key. Each key has its own charm, history, and adventures waiting to be had.

As a whole, Islamorada is known for its exciting activities. The group of islands is a popular destination for those interested in fishing, snorkeling, kayaking, and boating. Its fishing is particularly renowned. Many famous fishers have honed their craft on Islamorada, sometimes even inventing new types of fishing. Islamorada's fishing fame has earned it the title of the Sport-Fishing Capital of the World.

The name Islamorada is Spanish, translating to "purple isle."

Plantation Key

American Indians began living on Plantation Key around 500 CE. They built large mounds on the island. Europeans began settling on the key in the 1800s, stealing the land from the Indigenous people. Many of these settlers were farmers. The farmers grew large plantations of coconuts and pineapples. These crops were shipped north to the United States' East Coast.

> **There is no place in the world as beautiful.**[1]
> *—Marina owner Richard Stanczyk about Islamorada*

Today, Plantation Key is connected to the rest of the Keys by the Overseas Highway. The island has restaurants and weekly farmers markets. Visitors can stay at local hotels while exploring the scuba diving, snorkeling, and fishing that the key has to offer.

Windley Key

Southwest of Plantation Key lies Windley Key. Henry Flagler purchased this key in 1908. Flagler was building his railroad when he realized he would need more limestone. He found an abundance of the rock on Windley Key and opened a quarry. The island was used as a quarry until the 1960s.

Today, the quarry is part of Windley Key Fossil Reef Geological State Park. The park is open to visitors. A stroll through the quarry reveals coral fossils embedded in the stone walls. Tourists can make out cross sections of brain coral, star coral, and finger coral. Park visitors can see old mining machines scattered throughout the park. The park also contains trails leading into the key's tropical hardwood forest.

Abandoned Equipment

After the Overseas Railroad was completed, the limestone on Windley Key continued to be quarried. The stone was used to decorate buildings. Several of the machines that were used in this process are still in Windley Key Fossil Reef Geological State Park. The channeling machine, which cut grooves around blocks about to be removed, is perched on top of the quarry wall. The remains of the slabbing machine, which cut the limestone into slabs, and the gin pole, which lifted the limestone, are also within the quarry.

Upper Matecumbe Key

Farther southwest from Windley Key is Upper Matecumbe Key. This key is dotted with restaurants, museums, and resorts. One of its most popular attractions is the Keys History and Discovery Center. The museum is located within the Islander Resort and teaches visitors about Islamorada's past and present. The museum features an exhibit about sport fishing, artifacts from shipwrecks, and three aquariums designed to teach visitors about coral reef ecosystems. The center also has a small movie theater offering films on topics such as the Overseas Railroad and the 1935 Labor Day Hurricane.

Upper Matecumbe Key is also home to the Hurricane Monument. This monument honors those who

The Hurricane Monument was built in 1937.

died in the 1935 Labor Day Hurricane. Underneath the monument is a crypt containing the remains of more than 300 of the storm's victims, many of whom were World War I (1914–1918) veterans tasked with building bridges in the area.[2] The massive monument was built of Key limestone. Carved on the back is a map of the island chain.

Lower Matecumbe Key

Southwest of the upper island is Lower Matecumbe Key. The key's northeastern coast is home to Robbie's Marina. Visitors flock to the marina to arrange boat trips, park tours, fishing expeditions, snorkeling trips, and kayak rentals.

On the other end of the key is Anne's Beach. This small but beloved spot is named after local environmentalist Anne Eaton. The stretch of sand is narrow, so sunbathers and sandcastle builders have the most room at low tide.

Anne and Cyrus Eaton

Born in 1922, Anne Eaton began her journey toward environmentalism as a teacher. After she married a banker named Cyrus Eaton in 1957, the Eatons traveled around the globe, meeting some of the world's most prominent scientists. As they traveled, Cyrus managed the Cyrus Eaton Foundation. The foundation brought together scientists to support sustainability and social justice initiatives. Anne settled in the Florida Keys after her husband died. She passed away in 1992.

The beach's warm, shallow, blue waters are perfect for wading, and the lush mangroves allow for a little light exploration.

Those craving more activity can paddleboard, kayak, snorkel, and even kiteboard near the beach. People can also explore the beach's mangroves on foot. Between the beach's two parking lots, a quarter-mile (0.4 km) boardwalk with lookout points and picnic tables leads through the mangrove forest.[3]

Indian Key

Between the Lower and Upper Matecumbe Keys is Indian Key. This 11-acre (4 ha) island is a cultural and historical treasure, even being listed on the US National Register of Historic Places.[4] Today, the island is protected as Indian Key Historic State Park.

American Indians began living on Indian Key around 800 CE. When Europeans arrived, they settled on the island, displacing the native people. By 1829, there were about 50 residents on the island. They made money by fishing, catching turtles, and, most lucratively, wrecking. In 1831, John Jacob Housman bought Indian Key. He created his own wrecking business. Housman's business quickly flourished, and the island's economy flourished with it.

Indian Key is located about half a mile (0.8 km) offshore of Lower Matecumbe Key.

New businesses opened on the key, including a store, a hotel, warehouses, and wharves.

Housman's fortunes turned in 1840 when a Seminole man named Chakaika led a group of warriors in an attack on Indian Key. The group burned the island's buildings and killed many of the settlers. Housman escaped, but his wrecking operation was destroyed.

Over the next hundred years, Indian Key was used only intermittently. The US Navy used the island for shipbuilding, and Henry Flagler occupied the land during dredging operations. However, after the 1935 Labor Day

Hurricane swept through the Keys, Indian Key fell into complete disuse.

In 1971, the State of Florida bought Indian Key and designated it as a historic site. Today, tourists visit the island to walk the key's trails and see the abandoned town. Visitors can access the island by boat or kayak.

Indian Key's ghost town isn't the only place of interest on the island. Seagrass restoration is underway on the island. Seabirds including cormorants, ospreys, terns, gulls, and pelicans help the seagrass by visiting specially built stakes in the water and fertilizing the grass with their droppings. The seagrass helps make Indian Key, like so many of the Florida Keys, inviting to abundant sea life.

Off the southern shore of Indian Key is the San Pedro Underwater Archaeological Preserve State Park. This park protects the *San Pedro* shipwreck. The ship came from the Netherlands and sank during a hurricane in 1733. Its remains were discovered in 1960. Today, the remnants of the ship rest 18 feet (5 m) underwater.[5] Scuba divers and snorkelers can explore the site and view the ship's remaining ballast stones, small rocks that stabilize ships. Divers can also see replica cannons and an anchor that have been placed at the site to give tourists a sense of what the ship once looked like.

Lignumvitae Key

North of Indian Key is Lignumvitae Key. The key is named for the ancient tropical hardwood lignum vitae trees that populate the island. In 1919, the island was purchased by a wealthy chemist from Miami named William J. Matheson, who built a luxurious two-story home on the key. The mansion was decorated with Key limestone.

In 1971, Florida's government acquired the island. Today, the island is part of Lignumvitae Key Botanical State Park. The 287-acre (116 ha) park features a tropical hardwood hammock of lignum vitae trees.[6] It also protects Matheson's old home, which can be explored through self-guided or ranger-led tours.

Traveling Birds

More than 100 bird species migrate over the Florida Keys.[7] Some take a break on the mudflats or mangroves on the islands, while others just fly over. The birds range from the tiny northern parula to more than 16 species of raptors.[8] More peregrine falcons migrate through the Keys than anywhere else in the country. Some of these birds travel huge distances. The pectoral sandpiper travels from as far north as Siberia and Alaska to South America and back again.

CHAPTER
FIVE

THE MIDDLE KEYS

The Middle Keys are made of more than ten islands. As their name suggests, they are located in the middle of the Florida Keys. Each island has a unique history. Many of the Middle Keys are connected by the Overseas Highway. As one travels south along the highway, the expanses of water between the islands get longer. The final bridge as travelers head southwest through the Middle Keys is the great Seven Mile Bridge, which connects the Middle Keys to the Lower Keys.

In the center of the Middle Keys lies Marathon, a city made of more than a dozen islands. The city is sometimes affectionately called the Heart of the Keys. Marathon is a popular vacation spot and caters to families. People come to fish,

The Middle Keys are a popular destination for fishing, boating, and vacationing.

explore the ocean, and take in the beautiful scenery.

One particularly popular spot in Marathon is Sombrero Beach. Unlike most beaches in the Keys, this beach has soft white sand. This sand makes the beach a perfect nesting spot for sea turtles. From April through October, loggerhead sea turtles pull themselves ashore during the night to lay their eggs in the soft sand. City workers survey the beach carefully to look for nests and limit human activities in those areas.

Not-So-Sandy Beaches

When people think of beaches, they may picture soft sand. However, very few of the beaches along the Florida Keys coastline are sandy. The Keys' coral reefs act as a shield, protecting waves from crashing into the coastlines and causing the erosion that forms sandy beaches. The sand that does form is rough. It's made of limestone, aragonite, and fragments of corals, shells, and fossilized algae.

Crane Point Hammock is another popular attraction in Marathon. This nature reserve offers a variety of activities. Guests can begin their visit at the Orientation Hall with a nine-minute film discussing Crane Point Hammock's attractions. From there, visitors can explore the property on their own or sign up for a guided tour.

Crane Point Hammock's massive park offers something for everyone. Those interested in history can explore the Crane Point Museum, where exhibits include a 600-year-old dugout canoe and remains of pirate ships.

Those who enjoy seeing wildlife can explore the park's trails, walking down a boardwalk past an osprey nest and through a butterfly meadow.

Birdwatchers can visit the Marathon Wild Bird Center. Those looking for an adventure can contact the museum to book a kayaking trip or a snorkeling excursion. Visitors interested in a more unusual experience can dip their feet in the lagoon for a fish pedicure. The pool is full of tiny silver gambusia fish. When guests put their feet into the pool, the fish nibble on dead skin, leaving people feeling clean and fresh.

Long Key

The northernmost island in the Middle Keys is Long Key. A large portion of the island is home to Long Key State Park. This park is an excellent location for birdwatching. Herons, egrets, and ibis make their homes in the park, with migratory birds visiting the key seasonally.

What Is a Hammock?

Hammocks are tropical hardwood forest areas that are higher in elevation than the surrounding areas. They form a canopy that offers shade and provides a place for a wide variety of animals to live and thrive. The term originated from early inhabitants. They used the word *hammock* to mean a cool and shady place. After settlers arrived, the word was used to describe Florida's unique forests.

Golden silk orb-weaver spiders are often called banana spiders.

Birdwatchers might also spy threatened species such as the white-crowned pigeon or the spectacular pink roseate spoonbill.

Hikers come to Long Key State Park to walk along the Golden Orb Nature Trail. This trail was named after the golden silk orb-weaver spider. Once plentiful along the trail, these spiders became much rarer after the damage caused by Hurricane Irma in 2017. The Golden Orb Nature Trail leads through a hardwood hammock of tropical trees. The Layton Trail is another popular hiking trail in the park. This trail takes hikers through undisturbed mangrove forests, ending at Florida Bay.

The southernmost end of Long Key was once home to a luxury resort called the Long Key Fishing Camp. This camp was built by Henry Flagler in 1908. The camp was designed to appeal to the tourists who could now access the Keys with the help of the Overseas Railroad. Flagler's resort was destroyed by the 1935 Labor Day Hurricane. Today, the area offers a wide range of activities, including kayaking, hiking, fishing, and snorkeling. Stargazing is also popular among overnight campers. Long Key has low levels of light pollution, creating spectacular opportunities for looking at the stars.

Curry Hammock State Park

Far west of Long Key is Curry Hammock State Park. The park is the largest undeveloped piece of land between Key Largo and Big Pine Key. The island stretches between Grassy Key and Crawl Key. Curry Hammock State Park is named after Thomas Curry, a man who purchased large sections of land in the Upper and Middle Keys. His daughter fought for the land to be preserved. In 1991, her efforts led to the creation of the park.

Curry Hammock State Park is a prime spot for kayaking. Kayaks can be rented at the park. The park is also a popular hiking spot. The park's hiking trail goes through a tropical hardwood hammock and a mangrove swamp. Visitors in the fall months may spot large numbers of migrating peregrine falcons.

The Old Seven Mile Bridge

When the Key West Extension was damaged by the 1935 Labor Day Hurricane, the train's route was repurposed for the construction of the Overseas Highway. The stretch from Marathon to Pigeon Key, however, was converted to a walking and biking path. Today, the bridge is known as the Old Seven Mile Bridge. From the bridge's height, walkers can enjoy a bird's-eye view of marine life, including sharks, tarpon, and eagle rays. In 2016, the bridge was closed for construction. It opened again in January 2022. The bridge's reopening was attended by a crowd of fans.

Pigeon Key

West of Curry Hammock State Park is Pigeon Key. This island once housed the rail and maintenance laborers who worked to connect the Keys. From 1908 to 1912, during the most intense part of the construction of Flagler's Key West Extension, as many as 400 workers lived on Pigeon Key. The laborers worked ten hours a day, six days a week, making only $1.50 per day, or five dollars an hour in today's money.[1]

Today, the Pigeon Key Historic District has been declared a national historic landmark to protect the area where the workers lived. Visitors can explore the buildings that housed the railroad's workers. Those interested in learning more about the island's history can visit the

Pigeon Key can be accessed by boat or by walking, biking, or taking the train along the Old Seven Mile Bridge.

Assistant Bridge Tender's House. The building is now a museum dedicated to teaching visitors about Pigeon Key's rich history.

Pigeon Key has a number of other fun activities. Visitors can relax on the island's beach, snorkel in the surrounding waters, or fish. Those who are interested in feeding fish can take a trip to Pigeon Key's saltwater pool. The pool contains sharks, eels, and other marine creatures. Visitors can feed the animals in the afternoons.

> **If we decided we wanted to have a fresh fish for breakfast in the morning we'd run out and jump in the boat . . . and in five minutes we'd have fish.[2]**
>
> ***—Esther Hines Diver on her 1920s childhood on Pigeon Key***

CHAPTER SIX

THE LOWER KEYS

The Lower Keys are made of several islands. The islands in this section of the Keys include Big Pine Key, Bahia Honda Key, Looe Key, No Name Key, Sugarloaf Key, and Boca Chica Key. The islands extend from the west end of the Seven Mile Bridge to the edge of Key West.

Also called the Natural Keys, the Lower Keys are known for their beauty, both in their gorgeous landscapes and magnificent wildlife. The keys' occupants work hard to protect this beauty. The islands host marine sanctuaries, wildlife refuges, and a state park. Visitors can travel to the Lower Keys to visit the islands' awe-inspiring landscapes and natural wonders.

The Lower Keys are renowned for their tranquil beauty.

Bahia Honda Key

Bahia Honda Key is among the easternmost islands of the Lower Keys. The key is famous for Bahia Honda State Park. The park offers a wide variety of activities, including biking, hiking, and birdwatching. A walk on the park's nature trail will lead visitors to the top of Old Bahia Honda Bridge, from which visitors can see the entire island and, if the water is clear, fish and sea turtles swimming below.

No Name, No Electricity

No Name Key famously did not have any public electricity until May 2013. Residents used solar panels, windmills, and generators. A long and complicated legal battle with the local power company, which originally didn't want to run power cables due to the low population on the island, took decades to resolve.

Park guests can also enjoy the warm waters of the Calusa and Sandspur Beaches. The shallow waters make the beaches perfect for beginner snorkelers. The waters are also filled with beautiful marine life. Snorkelers may see soft corals, small coral heads, tropical fish, spiny lobsters, sea stars, and queen conchs.

There are plenty of other activities in the park's waterways. Some people come to the park to swim or fish. Others come to kayak or canoe, bringing their own or renting a watercraft from the park. Bahia Honda State Park is also an in-demand boating destination, as boaters

Don't Miss It!

Stargazing in Bahia Honda State Park

Daytime visitors to Bahia Honda State Park can enjoy sunlit experiences such as snorkeling among colorful fish and swimming in tropical blue waters. However, as the sun sets and stars appear against the twilight sky, Bahia Honda Key transforms into a glittering nighttime wonderland.

The Lower Keys are ideal for astronomers and stargazers due to their low light pollution. The night-sky viewing conditions are considered among the best in the United States, with Bahia Honda boasting the darkest skies for stargazing in the Florida Keys.

Nighttime visitors can pull up a chair and relax, taking in the sky and watching the sparkling show of stars and planets unfold above them. Some add to the magic by taking a walk under the starlight to the Old Bahia Honda Bridge or along the shore. It's a perfect chance to spot constellations. Because the park closes at sundown, only overnight guests can take advantage of this unique opportunity to see the night sky under such ideal conditions.

can access both the Gulf of Mexico and the Atlantic Ocean from the park.

With so much to explore, many choose to stay in the park overnight. The park offers three campgrounds and several deluxe cabins for campers. Reservations can be made in advance.

National Key Deer Refuge

Stretching over several of the Lower Keys, the National Key Deer Refuge works to protect the endangered Key deer. These tiny deer, a subspecies of the white-tailed

In the 1940s, human activity nearly drove Key deer to extinction.

deer, are found nowhere else in the world. Scientists estimate that there are only 1,000 Key deer left in existence.[1] The National Key Deer Refuge was established in 1957 to not only protect the deer but also to protect their habitats. Today, the refuge includes hammocks, mangrove forests, salt marshes, and freshwater wetlands.

> **It's not that the deer are endangered anymore. The habitat is endangered.[2]**
>
> ***—Nova Silvy, professor and wildlife researcher at Texas A&M University***

Tourists can visit the National Key Deer Refuge to look for Key deer. Many of the keys have trails for visitors to venture farther into the refuge. Lucky visitors may see Key deer along the trails or on the sides of roads. Deer may occasionally wander into the roads, so careful driving is essential.

Key Deer and Humans

As humans developed the Keys, much of the Key deer's habitat was destroyed, forcing the species closer to human towns. Over time, the deer became more accustomed to humans. Some humans began illegally feeding the deer, causing the deer to become further accustomed to and even dependent on humans. Today, many deer allow humans to approach them. Some even seek out humans, looking for food. This proximity to humans increases the risk of Key deer being attacked by pets, getting tangled in fences, and being hit by cars, further endangering the animals.

Though designed to protect Key deer, the refuge is home to many other animals too. Some of these animals live in the Blue Hole, a former quarry. After the quarry's abandonment, the hole filled with fresh water, becoming a lake. Native plants grew around the quarry, providing habitats for many species. Today, an observation platform allows visitors to view the diverse wildlife around the quarry. Animals that may make appearances include turtles, tarpon, and birds such as ospreys, green herons, and white-crowned pigeons. Some people even spot American alligators.

Looe Key

Looe Key is located five miles (8 km) south of Big Pine Key.[3] Despite its name, it is actually not a key. Instead, the island is a shallow coral reef. The island was named after

Winter Star Party

The low levels of light pollution on the Lower Keys provide stargazers with fantastic views of the night sky. This makes the region the perfect spot for the Winter Star Party. Every February since 1984, hundreds of amateur and professional astronomers have headed to the Lower Keys for a stargazing festival. The gathering is hosted by Miami's Southern Cross Astronomical Society (SCAS) and is open to both members of SCAS and the public. The weeklong party is filled with exciting events, including a traditional starlit walk on the beach, nightly stargazing, and lectures led by well-known astronomers.

HMS *Looe*, a ship that sank in 1744 when its rudder got stuck in the shallow reef.

Today, Looe Key is a part of the Florida Keys National Marine Sanctuary. People travel to the reef to snorkel. Guided snorkeling trips are available from Bahia Honda State Park.

Snorkelers may see several species of sharks around Looe Key, including blacktip reef sharks.

CHAPTER SEVEN

KEY WEST AND DRY TORTUGAS NATIONAL PARK

Key West is the last stop on the Overseas Highway. The key, along with several neighboring islands, forms the city of Key West, the southernmost city in the continental United States. At its southernmost point, the key is only 90 miles (145 km) from Cuba.[1]

Key West is filled with colorful homes, huge mansions, and lush gardens. The area is rich in history, with a fort, a state park, and museums honoring world-famous writers. The town is also steeped in tradition. One of the most famous and enduring practices in Key West is the nightly Sunset Celebration at the docks in Mallory Square.

Every day at sunset, the people of Key West flood the square to celebrate the

Key West's official motto is "One Human Family," a philosophy designed to promote unity.

end of another day on the island paradise. Townspeople mingle with tourists, watching musicians, acrobats, and other entertainers perform, while street vendors sell food to the crowd. The nightly gathering celebrates the unique wonder of Key West.

Famous Folk of Key West

Key West has had several famous residents. In the 1930s, author Ernest Hemingway moved to Key West. He lived in the city for almost ten years and loved the island. His novel *To Have and Have Not* was set in Key West. Today, the Ernest Hemingway Home and Museum at his former Key West residence is visited by thousands of people every year. Visitors can tour the author's Spanish colonial home and visit the studio where he wrote some of his most famous works.

> **"I think it's an intriguing place for people [to visit], because Hemingway did some of his greatest work here. He was at the peak of his powers here in Key West.[2]"**
>
> ***—Corey Malcom, lead historian for the Florida Keys History Center***

One of the most unusual features of the museum is the family of cats that freely roams the house. The cats are descended from Hemingway's cat Snow White. Many of the 60 resident cats are polydactyl, meaning they have one or two extra toes on some of their paws.

Famous playwright Tennessee Williams lived in Key West from 1941 until his death in 1983. He often stayed at La Concha Hotel, where it is believed he finished his play *A Streetcar Named Desire*. The Tennessee Williams Museum celebrates the playwright's time on the island. Visitors to the museum can see rare photographs of Williams, first editions of his plays and books, and the typewriter the author used while writing in Key West.

The historic Little White House, sometimes known as the Truman White House, also stands in Key West. During his time as the thirty-third US president, Harry S. Truman stayed in Key West for a total of about six months, acting as commander in chief from the former naval officer home at 111 Front Street. Visitors to the historic home can see the president's piano and poker table.

Key West Lighthouse

The Key West Lighthouse was built in 1848 after the US Navy established a base on the island. For more than 100 years, the lighthouse guided sailors to safety. The lighthouse was finally decommissioned in 1969. Today, the landmark serves as a museum. Guests can

The Key West Lighthouse was originally lit using oil made from whale blubber.

visit the lighthouse to learn about the brave people who maintained the light. Historic artifacts, photos, and journals on display tell the stories of courageous lighthouse keepers.

The lighthouse also offers a spectacular view of Key West. Visitors can climb the 88-step spiral staircase to the top of the tower.[3] An observation tower gives guests a 360-degree view of the beautiful island.

Fort Zachary Taylor Historic State Park

The southwestern tip of Key West is home to Fort Zachary Taylor Historic State Park. The park protects an old military fort built in 1845. During the American Civil War (1861–1865), Union troops used the fort to block ships from delivering supplies to the Confederacy.

Today, the park is an important historic site. Visitors can walk beside cannons, gun ports, and the largest collection of Civil War weapons in the country. There's a guided tour at the fort once a day, as well as a tour for park guests to take on their own. On the third weekend of every month, local reenactors stage re-creations of historic events, bringing them to life for onlookers and helping visitors understand the experiences of those who lived and worked at the fort.

Fort Zachary Taylor Historic State Park also has a wide range of other activities. The park has a wide, rocky beach that's perfect for swimming and snorkeling. Guests can bring their own snorkeling gear or rent gear from the park. Visitors can also explore the park's waterways by canoe or kayak. A boat launch for canoeing and kayaking is located at the east end of the park. Fishers can enjoy the park too, casting their lines off the rock jetty to reel in groupers, snappers, jacks, and tarpon.

Mel Fisher Maritime Museum

Mel Fisher spent his life searching for treasure around the Keys. He was specifically looking for sunken ships. Over decades of diving, Fisher recovered several shipwrecks. The most valuable was the *Nuestra Señora de Atocha*, a Spanish galleon that sank in a hurricane in 1622. Fisher found the ship 35 miles (56 km) west of Key West. The 1985 find yielded more than $400 million of gold, silver, and jewels.[4]

In 1987, Fisher used some of his profits to open the Mel Fisher Maritime Museum in Key West. Fisher's museum included exhibits about sunken ships, a research center, and conservation laboratories. Today, the museum houses artifacts from shipwrecks, allowing visitors to see and touch pieces of history. Pieces of four ships are also held in the museum, including the *Nuestra Señora de Atocha*, the *Santa Margarita*, and the *Santa Clara*. The treasures

In Memory of the *Henrietta Marie*

In 1992, the National Association of Black Scuba Divers (NABS) excavated the site of the *Henrietta Marie*. Divers were able to recover more than 7,000 objects from the wreck, making the ship the largest known source of artifacts of the early African slave trade. In 1993, the NABS placed a plaque at the shipwreck site. The plaque reads, "In memory and recognition of the courage, pain and suffering of enslaved African people. Speak her name and gently touch the souls of our ancestors."[5]

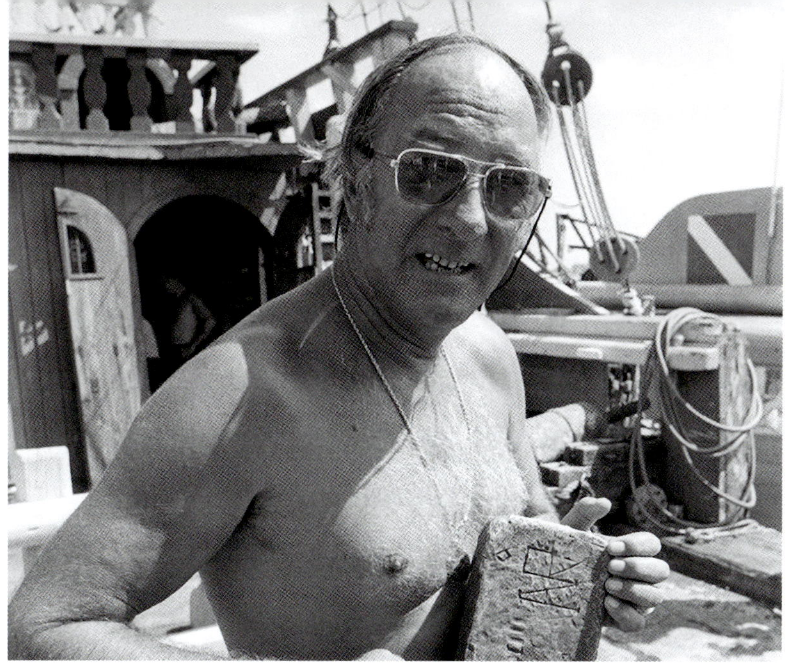

Mel Fisher spent more than 16 years searching for the *Nuestra Señora de Atocha*.

recovered from these ships included gold and silver bars, coins, tools, and weapons.

The fourth ship at the museum is the *Henrietta Marie*. Fisher located the ship in 1972. After examining the wreck, he realized that he had discovered a lost slaver ship. The *Henrietta Marie* had been used to kidnap African people and sell them into slavery. In 1700, the ship sank off the coast of Key West. Artifacts recovered from the ship included more than 80 pairs of shackles.[6]

Key West Butterfly and Nature Conservatory

South Key West is home to the Key West Butterfly and Nature Conservatory. Most visitors to the conservatory start their day at the Learning Center. This section of the conservatory gives visitors an introduction to the world of butterflies. A 15-minute film takes visitors through the life cycle of these spectacular creatures, while a mural on the wall maps out butterfly species by their country of origin and displays detailed illustrations of butterfly anatomy and physiology.

The centerpiece of the conservatory is a glass dome habitat that houses hundreds of butterflies and birds. Visitors can stroll among the lush tropical plants and crystal waterfalls. The scenery makes a perfect backdrop for at least 50 species of butterflies and a varied collection of brightly plumed birds.[7]

Inside the conservatory is an art studio where butterfly-themed art is displayed. Some of the art features real preserved butterflies, made with tropical butterflies that have lived out their natural lives. All the art is made on Key West. Visitors can purchase art as souvenirs of their time in the Keys.

The Key West Cemetery

A cemetery may seem like an unusual place to go for a laugh, but some Key West visitors do just that. The Key West Cemetery, established in 1847 and still actively used,

Key West Tropical Forest and Botanical Garden

In tourist-heavy Key West, it can be hard to find a place to relax. Visitors looking for a laid-back activity far from the island's busy commercial center can travel to the Key West Tropical Forest and Botanical Garden. Run by the Key West Botanical Garden Society, the garden focuses on biodiversity and the importance of sustaining native plant species in their natural habitats.

The garden's courtyard is packed with tropical plants. Hundreds of species of birds, butterflies, and flowers from the Keys, Cuba, and the Caribbean fill the 15.2-acre (6.2 ha) garden, which can be enjoyed via nature trails and boardwalks.[8] The garden features three freshwater ponds, a rarity in Key West, in which contented turtles lazily bask in the sun. And because the garden is along the migration path for many species of birds, visitors can spy migratory species coming from as far away as South America.

The garden also has educational exhibits, including a display of boats and rafts belonging to refugees. The boats, sometimes called Cuban chugs, carried people across the Straits of Florida to the United States.

is often visited for its humorous tombstones. "I told you I was sick," reads the headstone for B. P. Roberts. Gloria M. Russell's inscription reads, "I'm just resting my eyes."[9]

The cemetery is also rich with history. Many well-known Key Westerners are buried in the cemetery, such as Joseph S. "Sloppy Joe" Russell, Ernest Hemingway's favorite bartender. The cemetery is the final resting site for many veterans as well. It houses the memorial for the sailors killed in the 1898 explosion of the USS *Maine* in Cuba.

Dry Tortugas National Park

Founded in 1992, Dry Tortugas National Park is located about 70 miles (113 km) west of Key West. More than 99 percent of the park's 64,700 acres (26,200 ha) are underwater.[10] It's the least accessible national park in the United States, reachable only by a two-hour boat trip or a seaplane. This out-of-the-way location makes the area

Dry Turtles?

The islands in Dry Tortugas National Park were named Las Tortugas by Spanish explorer Juan Ponce de Leòn. *Tortuga* is the Spanish word for "turtle." The explorer named the islands after the sea turtles he saw in the surrounding waters. Sailors who later ventured past the keys found no fresh water on the islands and added "Dry" to the name to warn future travelers.

Dry Tortugas National Park is located in the Florida Keys National Marine Sanctuary.

perfect for snorkeling and scuba diving. Underwater explorers are often able to see more marine wildlife than anywhere else in the Keys.

A chain of seven small keys provides the only dry land in the park. The island chain is composed of the Bush, East, Garden, Hospital, Loggerhead, Long, and Middle Keys. Despite their small sizes, these keys played a large role in the region's history.

Garden Key

Garden Key played an especially important role in the creation of Dry Tortugas National Park. The key is the second-largest island in the park. In 1825, a lighthouse

Don't Miss It!

The Southernmost Point Buoy

On the corner of South and Whitehead Streets in Key West sits a giant concrete buoy. Permanently anchored to the spot, the massive monument is known as the Southernmost Point Buoy. The marker proclaims in painted lettering, "90 Miles to Cuba, Southernmost Point, Continental U.S.A."[11]

The monument was erected in 1983 by the City of Key West to combat theft. Previous simple signs marking the point kept being stolen. The giant concrete buoy, weighing at least 20 short tons (18 metric tons), was designed to be more difficult to steal.[12]

The buoy has needed repairs on several occasions. In 2017, the monument's paint was badly damaged in Hurricane Irma, and a local artist was commissioned to repaint it. The landmark has also endured some vandalism. On New Year's Day in 2022, two men set a Christmas tree on fire next to the buoy. City workers quickly initiated repairs, sanding and repainting the concrete. Today, the buoy is one of the most visited points in Key West.

was built on Garden Key to prevent ships from running aground. Years later, the military decided to place a fort on the island. By fortifying the island, the warships patrolling the Gulf of Mexico would have a safe place to dock. The base was named Fort Jefferson.

Construction on Fort Jefferson began in 1846 and continued for nearly 30 years. All the while, the fort was in use, first by Union forces during the Civil War, and then as a military prison. Much of the fort's construction was done by prisoners. The inmates worked under abysmal conditions. Between the forced labor and a deadly outbreak of yellow fever, Garden Key became known as Devil's Island.

After 1874, Fort Jefferson was used only minimally. In 1908, it was repurposed when President Theodore Roosevelt designated both the fort and the surrounding Dry Tortugas islands as a federal bird reservation. Today, the fort is preserved as a part of American history. Tourists come to the key to see the immense structure.

Though it was never completed, it remains one of the largest forts ever built. Visitors can explore Fort Jefferson on their own or on ranger-led guided tours. The tours take visitors around the structure, offering views of the fort's moat, structures for gunpowder storage, soldiers' barracks, and original guns weighing 25 short tons (23 metric tons).[13]

Park visitors can also explore the natural wonders of Garden Key. The key is the only place in Dry Tortugas National Park that allows camping. The key is also a great place for swimming, snorkeling, and scuba diving.

Fort Jefferson is the largest brick structure in the Americas.

Garden Key has three public swimming beaches, each named for its position on the key. The North, South, and East Beaches offer calm, shallow waters. Park guests can also snorkel in the waters around these beaches. Swimmers and snorkelers can search for old artifacts beneath the waves, such as anchor chains and cement barrels. People may also spot marine wildlife, including sharks, reef squid, and hogfish. Many animals are drawn to the area, as pilings left over from the dock provide homes for groupers, tarpon, and even barracuda.

Loggerhead Key

Loggerhead Key is another spectacular location for underwater exploration. The key offers fantastic swimming, snorkeling, and diving opportunities. Swimming and snorkeling are allowed off the northwest side of the key, where the waters are shallow and calm. This area is known for its fascinating coral formations.

One of the key's most famous coral formations is known as Little Africa. When viewed from above, this coral formation resembles the shape of the African continent. Loggerhead Key is also known for its wide array of marine wildlife. Swimmers and snorkelers may see young barracuda, lobsters, and tropical fish.

The *Avanti* was a commercial ship with multiple masts. These ships were known as windjammers, earning the wreck its nickname.

South of Loggerhead Key is the Windjammer shipwreck. This wreck is all that remains of the *Avanti*, a three-masted, iron-hulled vessel. In 1907, the *Avanti* was carrying lumber when it ran aground on Loggerhead Reef. The ship broke apart, scattering its remains across the seafloor. The wreck was discovered in 1971. Today, snorkelers and scuba divers can take a tour of the Windjammer shipwreck. Guests are invited to explore the wreck but must leave the remains untouched.

Unfortunately, few people are able to see Loggerhead Key's natural wonders, as this key can be challenging

to access. There are no public transport services to the key. This means that the island is accessible only by private boat.

Traveling to Dry Tortugas

Dry Tortugas can be hard to access. Some tourists boat to Dry Tortugas, though there is limited space for privately owned vessels. People without boats can take a ferry. However, the main ferry that takes people to Dry Tortugas has only ten seats. With dozens of people hoping to access the park daily, seats fill up months in advance. The ferry is also unable to transport dive tanks, so those intending to scuba dive need to arrange for a private boat to carry their gear. The area's inaccessibility might contribute to the park being one of the least visited national parks in the country.

CHAPTER EIGHT

ANIMALS OF THE KEYS

The Florida Keys are home to a wide range of fascinating creatures. From the region's mangrove trees to its multicolored coral reefs, the land is teeming with wildlife. More than 6,000 species live in the Florida Keys National Marine sanctuary alone.[1]

Many animals rely on the Keys to survive. In fact, several species are endemic to the Florida Keys. An endemic species is a species that can be found only in a single area. The biggest threats to these species are disease and habitat loss. Human development is the main cause of habitat loss in the Keys, but other factors such as natural disasters and rising sea levels can also endanger habitats, posing a risk to the region and its animals.

The Florida Keys are home to roughly 600 species of fish.

The Key Deer

One of the most famous species in the Florida Keys is the Key deer. The Key deer is the smallest subspecies of the white-tailed deer and is found only in the Florida Keys. Fully grown males weigh just 55 to 75 pounds (25 to 34 kg), with females weighing a little less. The shoulder height of these tiny deer is only 24 to 32 inches (61 to 81 cm).[2] Fawns are usually born between April and June. The deer give birth to only one fawn per year.

Key deer can be spotted at the National Key Deer Refuge headquartered on Big Pine Key in the Lower Keys. However, Key deer aren't the only rare animals that populate this refuge. Though it is rare for visitors to encounter them, American alligators, American crocodiles, and eastern diamondback rattlesnakes live in the Lower Keys too.

What Is Coral?

Rooted to the seafloor or stationary objects, corals may look like plants or colorful rocks. However, coral is actually made of thousands of tiny animals called polyps. Polyps are invertebrates, meaning they lack backbones. Each polyp contains a stomach. The stomach is open at one end and surrounded by tentacles that capture food. Providing habitats for hundreds of other animals, corals are among the most important animals in the Florida Keys.

The Lower Keys Marsh Rabbit

Marsh rabbits have small, gray-brown tails instead of the puffy tails seen on other types of rabbits. These animals are strong swimmers. The Lower Keys marsh rabbit is the smallest subspecies of marsh rabbit, growing to about 14 to 16 inches (36 to 41 cm) long.[3] They can be found in the area from Big Pine Key to Boca Chica Key.

Lower Keys marsh rabbits live in marshes. They make nests in places that offer some protection, such as thickets, stumps, or logs. The rabbits line the nests with grass and bits of their own fur to keep them cozy.

Key Largo Rodents

Two unique species of rodents can be found in the hammocks of Key Largo. The Key Largo woodrat is a skilled builder, making its home in North Key Largo's tropical hammock areas. This clever creature uses sticks to create large nests at the bases of trees and rocks.

Sharing the Key Largo hammocks with this woodrat is the Key Largo cotton mouse. This little creature nests in concealed areas such as logs, tree hollows, and rock crevices. It lines its nests with leaves. It comes out of its nest at night to eat fruits and seeds.

Florida Keys mole skinks have brightly colored tails.

The Florida Keys Mole Skink

The Florida Keys mole skink is a slim lizard that is brown, tan, or gray. It usually grows to a length of about five inches (13 cm).[4] These skinks are adept at burrowing, a skill that helps them live underground.

Mole skinks have been sighted on at least 23 of the Florida Keys.[5] They likely live elsewhere in the Keys, too, but have yet to be seen. The skinks inhabit sandy shorelines, making their homes under rocks, leaves, and driftwood.

Snails, Snakes, and Silversides

The Stock Island tree snail, once native to Stock Island and Key West, was declared extinct in its original habitats in 1992. However, small populations of this snail still exist in areas outside its historic habitats, especially in No Name Key and Key Largo. These snails are usually found in tropical hardwood hammocks, where they live in poisonwood, pigeon plum, Jamaican dogwood, strangler fig, and gumbo limbo trees.

The Key ringneck snake has been found in Key West, Big Pine Key, Little Torch Key, Middle Torch Key, and No Name Key. The snakes have gray-black backs and red-yellow underbellies. They eat insects, amphibians, and other snakes.

Key silversides are small fish endemic to the Lower and Middle Keys. At just two inches (5 cm) long, these fish can fit in the palm of a hand.[6] The fish earned their name from their bright silver color. They live in salt lagoons, eating small crustaceans and insects.

Tarpon

Tarpon are colossal fish, growing up to eight feet (2 m) long and weighing up to 280 pounds (130 kg).[7] Often called silver kings due to their massive size, these fish have existed since prehistoric times. They live in warm waters around Florida, the Gulf of Mexico, and the Caribbean. Every spring, thousands of tarpon migrate from the Gulf of Mexico and northern Florida toward the Keys. Fishers descend in droves to catch the massive fish. Enthusiasm for tarpon fishing has made the fish one of the most prized catches in Florida.

Even tourists without a passion for fishing can enjoy tarpon. Many visitors enjoy hand-feeding the enormous fish. Robbie's Marina in Islamorada is a popular spot for feeding the giants. A school of 100 tarpon gathers daily to be fed by Robbie's customers. Patrons can purchase a bucket of fish to feed the tarpon. Florida Keys Aquarium Encounters in Marathon and Sunset Marina in Key West offer more chances to feed tarpon.

Sharks

It's not unusual for people in the Keys to spot sharks while snorkeling in the shallow reefs. Sharks can often be found resting on the seafloor, where they feed on crustaceans and fish. The sharks usually do not threaten humans as long as their space is respected. However, sharks are wild animals, and visitors should be careful to maintain a safe distance. This decreases the likelihood that the animals will feel provoked.

If travelers crave a more interactive experience with sharks, the Keys offer several opportunities to safely get

Tarpon don't have sharp teeth, making them safe to feed.

closer to these animals. Nurse sharks and bull sharks occasionally join the tarpon off the docks at the Sunset Marina in Key West. Visitors can watch the sharks fight the tarpon for food. The Key West Aquarium offers guided tours that include feeding demonstrations for rays and sharks. Some guests get the opportunity to toss food to the sharks. The aquarium also includes a special tank where guides can assist visitors in handling queen conchs, sea stars, and other local marine animals.

Florida Manatees

The Florida Keys are home to a subspecies of manatee called the Florida manatee. Manatees are large marine mammals, averaging lengths of about nine to ten feet (3 m) and weighing about 1,000 pounds (450 kg). They have two flippers and a large paddle-shaped tail that help them move quickly through the water, allowing them to reach speeds of 15 miles per hour (24 kmh) for short amounts of time.[8] Manatees are vegetarians, living off of marine plants.

Florida manatees were once endangered, but by 2017, their population had rebounded enough for them to be reclassified as threatened. Despite the improvement, several dangers still put the species at risk. One of the primary dangers is the manatees' loss of habitat. This habitat loss is caused by human development on the coastline, which destroys the manatees' feeding areas. Waste from development also enters the water, causing algae blooms, some of which are poisonous to manatees. Manatees are also threatened by boat collisions. Speeding boats sometimes hit the creatures, killing or injuring them.

Baby manatees are called calves. Manatee calves stay with their mothers for up to two years.

Today, between 7,000 and 11,000 manatees inhabit Florida's waters.[9] They can be found in many state and national parks in the Keys, especially during the fall and winter. Although manatees can handle cooler temperatures, they prefer warmer weather, so they tend to head for the temperate climate of the Keys during the cooler months. Visitors who are kayaking, snorkeling, or swimming may occasionally spot the majestic creatures. Those eager to see manatees can visit John Pennekamp Coral Reef State Park, Indian Key Historic State Park, Dry Tortugas National Park, or Biscayne National Park.

Sea Turtles

The Florida Keys are home to five species of sea turtles.[10] These species are the loggerhead, green, leatherback, hawksbill, and Kemp's ridley sea turtles. All five species are endangered or threatened.

Years ago, turtles were plentiful in the Keys' waters. Now, sightings are much less frequent. Conservationists are working hard to restore sea turtle populations. Visitors can help in these efforts by respecting the

> **I look at every turtle as something special. I love them all.[11]**
>
> ***—Richie Moretti, founder of a turtle hospital in Marathon***

The Turtle Hospital

The Turtle Hospital in Marathon tends to sick and injured sea turtles. The hospital has nursed more than 3,000 sea turtles back to health.[12] The staff treats many ailments, such as intestinal problems caused by turtles eating trash, shell damage from boat collisions, injuries from getting tangled in fishing gear, and disease. Tourists can visit the hospital to learn more about sea turtle conservation. The hospital also offers 90-minute programs that include a behind-the-scenes look at turtle care and a chance to feed some of the hospital's turtles.

wild animals' space. It's illegal to harass any endangered species. Even shining an artificial light on sea turtles can count as harassment, as it disorients them. Threats to sea turtles include being caught in fishing nets, being hit by boats, and ingesting or becoming tangled in plastic waste.

Crocodile Lake National Wildlife Refuge

The endangered American crocodile lives in the Florida Keys National Marine Sanctuary. It also has a sanctuary at Crocodile Lake National Wildlife Refuge on Key Largo. Here, crocodiles make their homes in saltwater mangroves.

The area also contains hammock forests that support other rare animals. The Stock Island tree snail, Schaus' swallowtail butterfly, and the eastern indigo snake have all been sighted in the Crocodile Lake National

American crocodiles can live up to 70 years in the wild.

Wildlife Refuge. Most of the refuge isn't open to the public, though tourists can visit a small butterfly sanctuary located in the area.

Crocodiles and Alligators

Crocodiles and alligators are reptiles from the crocodilian group, a group containing the largest living reptiles. Only two species from this group are native to the United States, and South Florida is the only place with both of them.[13] While the species may look similar at first glance, the animals have distinct differences. Crocodiles have muscular tails, gray-green backs, and triangular snouts. They live in coastal, brackish, and saltwater habitats. Alligators have broader snouts. They prefer freshwater habitats.

SPORTS IN THE KEYS

The Florida Keys offer a wide range of outdoor activities. Biking is popular, especially on the Florida Keys Overseas Heritage Trail and other scenic routes. Fishing is another popular activity. World-class fishing brings anglers to the Keys' waterways, where they search for tarpon and other big game fish.

Many tourists explore the ocean. Boating and sailing are available throughout the keys. Kayaking offers a serene experience and brings paddlers close to local wildlife. Snorkeling, swimming, and scuba diving allow adventurers to explore coral reefs and underwater parks. Each activity gives tourists a unique view of the Florida Keys.

Some parts of the Florida Keys have marked kayaking trails.

Biking

The Florida Keys are home to some of the most beautiful biking trails in the country. Visitors can bring their own bikes to the Keys or rent bikes upon arrival. Bikes are available for rent in a number of cities, including Key Largo, Islamorada, Marathon, and Key West.

A Trail across the Keys

The Overseas Heritage Trail was intended to be a multiuse trail stretching from Key Largo to Key West. However, a continuous paved trail across the Keys that is safe for bicyclists remains a distant goal. Damage from Hurricane Irma in 2017 halted progress, even temporarily closing the trail. While the official plans for completion still exist, work had not resumed by 2024.

Many trails in the Keys can be traveled by bike, providing visitors with a fun way to explore the island chain. For a trip back in time, cyclists can bike the 2.2-mile (3.5 km) stretch of the Old Seven Mile Bridge over the water from Marathon to Pigeon Key.[1] While in Marathon, visitors can bike along Sombrero Beach Road to the idyllic Sombrero Beach.

A rewarding way to explore the Florida Keys is by biking parts of the Florida Keys Overseas Heritage Trail. The Overseas Heritage Trail is a 106-mile (171 km) pathway through the Keys. The trail itself isn't bikeable in all places, but 90 miles (145 km) of it is.[2] The biking trail includes

23 bridges left from the Overseas Railroad. The trail forms a continuous, 20-mile (30 km) path on Key Largo, while trails on Grassy Key wind through mangroves.[3]

Fishing

The Florida Keys are famous for the world-class fishing available off the islands' shores. The Atlantic Ocean lies off the east and south coasts of the Keys,

Fishers can protect the Florida Keys' biodiversity by releasing the fish they catch.

providing ideal areas for sport fishing. Fishers in these areas look for high-energy catches such as marlins, sailfish, and swordfish. Offshore, fishers cast their lines into deeper waters, searching for bluefish and mahi-mahi. The north and west coasts open toward the Gulf of Mexico and Florida Bay, offering calmer waters. These areas have prized game fish such as bonefish, tarpon, permit, redfish, and snook.

Bridges can be great spots to catch fish. Fishing is allowed off the Old Seven Mile Bridge in Marathon and the Long Key Viaduct Bridge, while onshore fishing is allowed in Bahia Honda State Park. Fort Zachary Taylor Historic State Park allows fishing off a rock jetty. Fishing licenses may be required, so fishers should always check local regulations before casting their lines.

> **“When I'm not fishing in the Florida Keys, I am thinking about my next trip and about how great the last one was.[4]**
>
> ***—Harold Morlan, frequent fisher in Islamorada”***

Boating and Sailing

Thousands of boaters visit the Florida Keys every year to enjoy the archipelago's beautiful waterways. Those without their own boats can rent vessels from commercial ventures throughout the Keys. However, all boaters should be knowledgeable and well trained. Boating in the Keys can be challenging, especially for those unfamiliar with navigating the shallow waters around the islands. Even experienced boaters face difficulties, with many vessels running aground on seagrass beds, tidal flats, and coral reefs.

Officials in the Keys emphasize the importance of safe boating. Carelessness not only puts human lives at risk but also can harm the Keys' fragile ecosystem. Running aground can damage seagrass beds and coral reefs. This can destroy habitats that animals throughout the Keys depend on, putting marine life in danger.

Kayaking

The Florida Keys' waters can be very shallow near the shores, with many areas accessible only by small watercraft such as kayaks. Kayaking opportunities are available up and down the Keys, perfect for exploring mangrove tunnels and lagoons. In some areas, kayaks are available for rent. In others, visitors must bring their own kayaks. Many businesses offer guided kayaking tours, taking visitors through the Keys' most beautiful waterways.

John Pennekamp Coral Reef State Park, with its colorful reefs and mangrove forests, is a particularly spectacular area for kayaking. Plenty of other parks allow kayaking, including Biscayne National Park, Long Key State Park, Indian Key Historic State Park, Curry Hammock State Park, Crane Point Hammock, and Bahia Honda State Park. Lucky kayakers in these areas may spot a manatee. The winter season is best for kayaking, allowing visitors to avoid the brunt of the summer heat.

Kayaking the Keys

Kayaking allows tourists to explore portions of the Florida Keys that are inaccessible by foot. The sport also offers a way to silently observe the amazing wildlife around the Keys. Gliding quietly through mangrove forests, kayakers can encounter manatees, stingrays, birds, and even sharks. Today, kayaking is so popular that some hotels in the Keys include kayaks in their room prices. Many towns in the region accommodate kayakers too, with dozens of publicly accessible boat ramps available in the Keys.

Swimming, Snorkeling, and Scuba Diving

With two national parks and two state parks that are almost entirely underwater, swimming, snorkeling, and scuba diving are among the best ways to explore the Florida Keys. The kaleidoscope of coral reefs throughout the Florida Keys is never far from the islands. Getting into the water is a great way to explore the reefs and the life that thrives in and around them. The underwater world just below the surface of mangrove forests offers amazing sights as well.

It's up to the traveler to choose how to explore the Keys' underwater wonders. Each activity has its own benefits. While swimming is the simplest and requires no specialized equipment, it does limit the sites tourists are able to explore, as swimmers are able to stay underwater for only short periods of time.

However, there are still plenty of attractions that swimmers can see, such as shallow coral reefs, bright fish, and even a few shipwrecks. Swimming can also be a fun way to explore the Keys' beaches. Beaches on the Keys tend to be more rocky than soft and sandy, but there are still many fantastic swimming spots. Sandy beaches include Anne's Beach and Sombrero Beach.

Most people who can swim can learn to snorkel. Many can learn in less than an hour, though the Professional Association of Diving Instructors (PADI) offers a more involved course. Visitors can bring their own snorkeling equipment or rent equipment from many of the Keys' parks. Snorkeling allows visitors to comfortably remain under shallow water, letting them better take in the

Snorkeling is a great way to see the Florida Keys' rich wildlife.

gorgeous world under the surface. Many of the Keys' coral reefs and several of the region's shipwrecks can be explored by snorkeling.

Scuba diving gives visitors the greatest amount of freedom in the Keys. Divers can stay underwater for extended periods of time, exploring otherwise inaccessible areas of the region. These areas include the Keys' deep shipwrecks. However, scuba diving takes time and money to learn. A certification, sometimes called an open-water certification, is required to scuba dive.

Those who want to get their certificates must complete classroom work, pool diving training, and open-water dives. Scuba students should allow three to five days for the training. The price varies, but aspiring divers should expect to pay at least a few hundred dollars. There are professional PADI dive centers on Key Largo, Islamorada, and Key West.

The Florida Keys are among the most beautiful natural areas in the world. Teeming with plant life, marine animals, and fascinating stories, the Keys are unique for both their biodiversity and their history. Visitors who get the chance to set foot on the Florida Keys will never forget their awe-inspiring experiences.

Diana Nyad

In 2013, marathon swimmer Diana Nyad came ashore at Smathers Beach in Key West after a 53-hour, 111-mile (180 km) swim from Havana, Cuba. At age 64, she became the first person to accomplish this feat without a shark cage. Ten years later, Nyad celebrated her accomplishment by releasing Rocky, a rescued sea turtle, back into the ocean. The 120-pound (50 kg) sea turtle was being released after undergoing surgery and months of recovery at the Florida Keys Turtle Hospital.[5]

ESSENTIAL FACTS

FLORIDA KEYS BASICS

- The Florida Keys are a coral, limestone, and sandbar island chain trailing westward off the southern tip of Florida.
- The Keys have been occupied since prehistoric times. Europeans first arrived on the island chain in 1513.
- The Florida Keys include two national parks and ten state parks. These preserved areas have abundant natural beauty.
- The Keys have a rich maritime history that can be explored through the shipwrecks submerged in their waters and the landmarks and museums on the Keys' islands.

THINGS TO SEE AND DO

- Take a trip on a glass-bottom boat to Molasses Reef to see the undersea wildlife in John Pennekamp Coral Reef State Park.
- Swim or snorkel to the shipwreck artifacts off Cannon Beach.
- Kayak to the ruins of a once-thriving wrecking settlement at Indian Key Historic State Park.
- Fish off the Old Seven Mile Bridge in Marathon.
- Bike part of the Overseas Heritage Trail across the Keys.
- Visit the National Key Deer Refuge in the Lower Keys.
- Explore historic Fort Jefferson in Dry Tortugas National Park.

MAP

QUOTE

"It's the best place I've ever been any time, anywhere."

—*Author Ernest Hemingway on Key West*

GLOSSARY

biodiversity

The many different plants and animals in an ecosystem.

conservatory

A structure in which plants are protected and displayed.

coral head

A rounded hump or projection on or close to the submerged portion of a coral reef.

dredging

The process of removing material from the bottoms of waterways to allow boats to safely travel.

ecotourist

A traveler who practices ecotourism, a form of tourism that encourages traveling responsibly and conserving the natural environment.

endangered

At risk of becoming extinct.

hard coral

Coral with calcium carbonate skeletons.

key

An island formed by an ancient coral reef.

marine sanctuary

A special area designated by the National Oceanic and Atmospheric Administration to protect ocean ecosystems.

maritime

Having to do with the sea or waterways.

nomadic

Moving from one place to another.

seagrass

Flowering plants that live in shallow coastal waters.

soft coral

Coral that does not have a calcium carbonate skeleton.

threatened

Referring to a species that is considered likely to become endangered in the foreseeable future.

tunicate

A marine animal without a backbone that attaches to docks, rocks, and the bottoms of boats.

ADDITIONAL RESOURCES

SELECTED BIBLIOGRAPHY

Davenport, Fionn, et al. *Florida*. 9th ed., Lonely Planet, 2021.

Ham, Anthony, et al. *Miami and the Keys*. 9th ed., Lonely Planet, 2021.

National Geographic Guide to National Parks of the United States. 9th ed., National Geographic, 2021.

FURTHER READINGS

Hand, Carol. *Marine Conservation*. Abdo, 2025.

McDougall, Peter, et al. *Florida Keys*. Reef Smart Guides, 2022.

Top 10 Miami and the Keys. DK, 2023.

ONLINE RESOURCES

To learn more about the Florida Keys, please visit **abdobooklinks.com** or scan this QR code. These links are routinely monitored and updated to provide the most current information available.

MORE INFORMATION

For more information on this subject, contact or visit the following organizations:

FLORIDA KEYS NATIONAL MARINE SANCTUARY

33 E. Quay Rd.
Key West, FL 33040
floridakeys.noaa.gov

The Florida Keys National Marine Sanctuary is protected by the National Oceanic and Atmospheric Administration. The sanctuary's website provides information about the Florida Keys, activities to enjoy in the region, and ways to protect the marine environment.

KEY LARGO CHAMBER OF COMMERCE AND FLORIDA KEYS VISITOR CENTER

106000 Overseas Hwy.
Key Largo, FL 33037
keylargochamber.org

The Key Largo Chamber of Commerce and Florida Keys Visitor Center offers free brochures and a visitor's guide listing the many attractions and businesses in Key Largo. The organization can also help visitors book lodging.

LIBRARY OF FLORIDA HISTORY

435 Brevard Ave.
Cocoa, FL 32922
myfloridahistory.org/library

Part of the Florida Historical Society, the Library of Florida History preserves items such as books, maps, postcards, photographs, and documents that bring Florida's history to life.

SOURCE NOTES

CHAPTER 1. THE ISLAND CHAIN

1. "Florida Keys." *Britannica*, n.d., britannica.com. Accessed 18 Nov. 2024.

2. "Key West City Information." *Key West City*, 4 Feb. 2006, web.archive.org. Accessed 18 Nov. 2024.

3. Melissa Coleman. "36 Hours in Key West, Fla." *New York Times*, 29 Apr. 2015, nytimes.com. Accessed 18 Nov. 2024.

4. "Seminole History." *Florida Department of State*, n.d., dos.fl.gov. Accessed 18 Nov. 2024.

5. "Florida Keys—History." *Florida Fish and Wildlife Conservation Commission*, n.d., myfwc.com. Accessed 18 Nov. 2024.

6. "The Flagler Railroad." *Florida State Parks*, n.d., floridastateparks.org. Accessed 18 Nov. 2024.

7. "The 15 Worst Hurricanes in Florida Keys History." *National Oceanic and Atmospheric Administration*, n.d., noaa.maps.arcgis.com. Accessed 18 Nov. 2024.

8. Tracey Teo. "The Overseas Highway: The US' 'Floating' Highway." *BBC*, 24 May 2024, bbc.com. Accessed 18 Nov. 2024.

9. "Florida Keys," *Britannica*.

10. "Creature Feature." *Florida Keys National Marine Sanctuary*, n.d., floridakeys.noaa.gov. Accessed 18 Nov. 2024.

11. "Florida Keys," *Britannica*.

12. "Florida Keys." *Earth Is Blue Magazine*, n.d., sanctuaries.noaa.gov. Accessed 18 Nov. 2024.

13. "Florida Keys National Marine Sanctuary: Establishment of Temporary Special Use Area for Coral Nursery." *National Oceanic and Atmospheric Administration*, 27 June 2024, federalregister.gov. Accessed 18 Nov. 2024.

CHAPTER 2. THE NORTHERNMOST KEYS

1. "Boca Chita Key." *National Park Service*, 29 Dec. 2023, nps.gov. Accessed 18 Nov. 2024.

2. "Plan Your Visit." *National Park Service*, 17 Aug. 2022, nps.gov. Accessed 18 Nov. 2024.

3. "The South Florida Reef Ambassador Initiative." *Florida Department of Environmental Protection*, 13 Dec. 2024, floridadep.gov. Accessed 8 Jan. 2025.

4. "What Are Christmas Tree Worms?" *National Oceanic and Atmospheric Administration*, 17 Nov. 2020, oceanservice.noaa.gov. Accessed 18 Nov. 2024.

5. "Biscayne National Park." *National Park Service History eLibrary*, 30 Sept. 2024, npshistory.com. Accessed 18 Nov. 2024.

6. "Erl King." *National Park Service*, 28 Apr. 2021, nps.gov. Accessed 18 Nov. 2024.

7. "Lugano." *National Park Service*, 28 Apr. 2021, nps.gov. Accessed 18 Nov. 2024.

CHAPTER 3. KEY LARGO

1. "Florida Keys." *Britannica*, n.d., britannica.com. Accessed 18 Nov. 2024.

2. "History." *Florida State Parks*, n.d., floridastateparks.org. Accessed 18 Nov. 2024.

3. "Dagny Johnson Key Largo Hammock Botanical State Park." *Florida State Parks*, n.d., floridastateparks.org. Accessed 18 Nov. 2024.

4. "Dagny Johnson Key Largo Hammock Botanical State Park."

5. "Florida Keys."

6. Richard Dawkins. "Of Mind and Matter: David Attenborough Meets Richard Dawkins." *Guardian,* 10 Sept. 2010, theguardian.com. Accessed 18 Nov. 2024.

7. "Glassbottom Boat Tours." *John Pennekamp Coral Reef State Park*, n.d., pennekamppark.com. Accessed 18 Nov. 2024.

8. "Experiences and Amenities." *Florida State Parks*, n.d., floridastateparks.org. Accessed 18 Nov. 2024.

9. "How to Visit Christ of the Abyss from Key Largo & Islamorada." *SeaEO,* n.d., sea-eo.com. Accessed 18 Nov. 2024.

10. "Experiences and Amenities."

11. "Mangrove Forest." *Florida Keys National Marine Sanctuary*, n.d., floridakeys.noaa.gov. Accessed 18 Nov. 2024.

12. "Laura Quinn Wild Bird Sanctuary." *Florida Keys Wild Bird Center*, n.d., keepthemflying.org. Accessed 18 Nov. 2024.

CHAPTER 4. ISLAMORADA

1. Charles Greenfield. "The Moorings Village: FL Keys Coolest Resort." *Famtripper,* 2016, famtripper.com. Accessed 18 Nov. 2024.

2. Jill Zima Borski. "Remembering the Labor Day Hurricane." *Keys Life Magazine*, n.d., keyslifemagazine.com. Accessed 18 Nov. 2024.

3. "Anne's Beach." *Lonely Planet,* n.d., lonelyplanet.com. Accessed 18 Nov. 2024.

4. "Indian Key Historic State Park." *Trail of Florida's Indian Heritage*, n.d., trailoffloridasindianheritage.org. Accessed 18 Nov. 2024.

5. "Discover 10 State Parks in the Florida Keys & Key West." *Florida Keys and Key West*, 30 May 2017, fla-keys.com. Accessed 18 Nov. 2024.

6. "Florida Keys State Parks Offer Wide-Open Spaces, Expansive Scenery." *Florida Keys and Key West*, 22 Sept. 2020, fla-keys.com. Accessed 18 Nov. 2024.

7. "Bird Migration in the Florida Keys FAQ." *National Weather Service*, n.d., weather.gov. Accessed 18 Nov. 2024.

8. "Spring Migration." *National Weather Service*, n.d., weather.gov. Accessed 18 Nov. 2024.

SOURCE NOTES CONTINUED

CHAPTER 5. THE MIDDLE KEYS

1. Jeff Klinkenberg. "The Florida Keys: Seven Mile Bridge." *Visit Florida*, n.d., visitflorida.com. Accessed 18 Nov. 2024.

2. Thomas Neil Knowles. "The Crossing at Knights Key and the Island Community of Pigeon Key." *Florida Keys Sea Heritage Journal*, vol. 21, no. 2, 2011, keywestmaritime.org. Accessed 18 Nov. 2024.

CHAPTER 6. THE LOWER KEYS

1. "Key Deer." *National Wildlife Federation*, n.d., nwf.org. Accessed 18 Nov. 2024.

2. Nathan Rott and Ryan Kellman. "A Tiny Deer and Rising Seas: How Far Should People Go to Save an Endangered Species?" *NPR*, 12 Nov. 2023, npr.org. Accessed 18 Nov. 2024.

3. "Looe Key National Marine Sanctuary." *Lonely Planet,* n.d., lonelyplanet.com. Accessed 18 Nov. 2024.

CHAPTER 7. KEY WEST AND DRY TORTUGAS NATIONAL PARK

1. "Only 90 Miles from Cuba." *Florida Keys and Key West*, 5 Aug. 2019, fla-keys.com. Accessed 18 Nov. 2024.

2. Nancy Stetson. "Hemingway's Historic Home." *Florida Weekly*, 15 Aug. 2024, keywest.floridaweekly.com. Accessed 18 Nov. 2024.

3. "Present-Day Sites Bring Keys' Past to Life." *Florida Weekly*, 12 Mar. 2023, keywest.floridaweekly.com. Accessed 18 Nov. 2024.

4. "'Silver' Anniversary of Key West's Golden Treasure Hoard." *Florida Keys and Key West*, 16 July 2010, fla-keys.com. Accessed 18 Nov. 2024.

5. Janie Hubbard. "Inquiry: Tragic Journeys of Enslaved African People Exposed through Shipwreck Archaeology." *Councilor: A Journal of the Social Studies*, vol. 82, no. 2, May 2021, thekeep.eiu.edu. Accessed 18 Nov. 2024.

6. "The Henrietta Marie an English Merchant Slave Ship, Wrecked 1700." *Mel Fisher Maritime Museum*, n.d., melfisher.org. Accessed 18 Nov. 2024.

7. "Explore." *Key West Butterfly and Nature Conservatory*, n.d., keywestbutterfly.com. Accessed 18 Nov. 2024.

8. "Home." *Key West Tropical Forest & Botanical Garden*, n.d., keywest.garden. Accessed 18 Nov. 2024.

9. "The Plot Thickens at the Key West Cemetery." *Marker*, 2 Nov. 2020, themarkerkeywest.com. Accessed 18 Nov. 2024.

10. "This National Park Is a Haven for Turtles." *National Geographic*, 5 Nov. 2009, nationalgeographic.com. Accessed 18 Nov. 2024.

11. "Key West's Southernmost Buoy." *Key West Express*, 22 Mar. 2021, keywestexpress.net. Accessed 18 Nov. 2024.

12. Jeff Kleinman. "How Did Key West End Up with a Giant Buoy as a Tourist Attraction? Here's the Story." *Miami Herald*, 18 Mar. 2024, miamiherald.com. Accessed 18 Nov. 2024.

13. "Fort Jefferson Tour." *Dry Tortugas National Park and Fort Jefferson Ferry Service*, n.d., drytortugas.com. Accessed 18 Nov. 2024.

CHAPTER 8. ANIMALS OF THE KEYS

1. "Creature Feature." *Florida Keys National Marine Sanctuary*, n.d., floridakeys.noaa.gov. Accessed 18 Nov. 2024.

2. "Key Deer." *National Wildlife Federation*, n.d., nwf.org. Accessed 18 Nov. 2024.

3. "Lower Keys Rabbit." *Florida Fish and Wildlife Conservation Commission*, n.d., myfwc.com. Accessed 18 Nov. 2024.

4. "Florida Keys Mole Skink." *US Fish & Wildlife Service*, n.d., fws.gov. Accessed 18 Nov. 2024.

5. "Florida Keys Mole Skink."

6. "Key Silverside." *Florida Fish and Wildlife Conservation Commission*, n.d., myfwc.com. Accessed 18 Nov. 2024.

7. "Tarpon Facts." *Florida Fish and Wildlife Conservation Commission*, n.d., myfwc.com. Accessed 18 Nov. 2024.

8. "Manatee." *US Fish & Wildlife Service*, n.d., fws.gov. Accessed 18 Nov. 2024.

9. Christian Thorsberg. "Nearly 1,000 Manatees Converge on Florida State Park to Keep Warm in Record-Breaking Sighting." *Smithsonian*, 30 Jan. 2024, smithsonianmag.com. Accessed 18 Nov. 2024.

10. "Sea Turtles." *National Park Service*, 4 Jun. 2017, nps.gov. Accessed 18 Nov. 2024.

11. Josie Gulliksen. "Richie Moretti, Turtle Champion." *Josie Gulliksen*, 17 May 2020, josiegulliksen.com. Accessed 18 Nov. 2024.

12. "About Us." *Turtle Hospital*, 2023, turtlehospital.org. Accessed 18 Nov. 2024.

13. "American Crocodile: Species Profile." *National Park Service*, 7 Sept. 2023, nps.gov. Accessed 18 Nov. 2024.

CHAPTER 9. SPORTS IN THE KEYS

1. "A Short History of the Old Seven Mile Bridge." *Pigeon Key*, 21 Jan. 2022, pigeonkey.net. Accessed 18 Nov. 2024.

2. "Florida Keys Overseas Heritage Trail." *Florida State Parks*, n.d., floridastateparks.org. Accessed 18 Nov. 2024.

3. "Biking the Florida Keys Overseas Heritage Trail." *Florida State Parks*, n.d., floridastateparks.org. Accessed 18 Nov. 2024.

4. "Planning the Perfect Florida Keys Fishing Trip." *FishAnywhere.com*, n.d., fishanywhere.com. Accessed 18 Nov. 2024.

5. "Diana Nyad to Mark 10th Anniversary of Epic Cuba-to-Key West Swim with Oct. 22 Turtle Release." *Florida Keys and Key West*, 18 Oct. 2023, fla-keys.com. Accessed 18 Nov. 2024.

INDEX

Anne's Beach, 39–40, 97

Bahia Honda Key, 52, 54, 55, 56, 59, 94, 96
Big Pine Key, 49, 52, 58, 80, 81, 83
Biscayne Bay, 19, 20, 21
Biscayne National Park, 11, 13, 14, 18–23, 87, 96
Boca Chita Key, 16, 18–19
Bush Key, 71

Calusa Beach, 54
Calusa nation, 6–7
Cannon Beach, 30, 31–32
Chekika, 41
Coe, Ernest, 15
Crane Point Hammock, 7, 46–47, 96
Crawl Key, 49
Creek Nation, 8
Crocodile Lake National Wildlife Refuge, 86–87
Cuba, 6, 60, 69, 70, 72, 99
Curry Hammock State Park, 49, 50, 96

Dagny Johnson Key Largo Hammock Botanical State Park, 24–26
Douglas, Marjory Stoneman, 15
Dry Tortugas National Park, 11, 13, 14, 70–71, 73–77, 87

East Beach, 75
East Key, 71
Eaton, Anne, 39
Eaton, Cyrus, 39
Elliott Key, 16, 18–19
enslaved people, 8, 66, 67
Everglades National Park, 15, 24

Far Beach, 32
Fisher, Mel, 66–67
Flagler, Henry, 11, 36, 41, 49, 50
Florida Keys National Marine Sanctuary, 11, 13–14, 59, 78, 88
Florida Keys Wild Bird Center, 32–33
Florida Reef, 14, 19
Foley, Robert, 32
Fort Jefferson, 73–74
Fort Zachary Taylor Historic State Park, 65, 94

Garden Key, 71, 73–75
Glades Culture, 6
Grassy Key, 49, 93

Hemingway, Ernest, 6, 62–63, 70
Hospital Key, 71
Housman, John Jacob, 40–41
Hurricane Irma, 11, 48, 72, 92
Hurricane Monument, 38–39

Indian Key, 10, 34, 40–42, 43, 87, 96

John Pennekamp Coral Reef State Park, 13, 26–32, 87, 96

Key Largo, 14, 15, 17, 24–33, 49, 81, 83, 88–89, 92, 93, 99
Key West, 6, 10, 11, 14, 15, 17, 50, 52, 60–70, 72, 82–83, 84, 85, 92, 99
Key West Butterfly and Nature Conservatory, 67–68
Key West Cemetery, 68, 70
Key West Tropical Forest and Botanical Garden, 69

Lignumvitae Key, 34, 43
Little Torch Key, 83
Loggerhead Key, 71, 75–77
Long Key, 47–49, 71, 94, 96
Looe Key, 52, 58–59
Lower Matecumbe Key, 34, 39–40

Marathon, Florida, 7, 44–47, 50, 84, 87, 88, 92, 94
Maritime Heritage Trail, 11, 21–23
Matheson, William J., 43
Mel Fisher Maritime Museum, 66–67
Meredith, James, 11
Middle Key, 71
Middle Torch Key, 83

National Key Deer Refuge, 56–58, 80
1935 Labor Day Hurricane, 11, 12, 38–39, 41–42, 49, 50
No Name Key, 15, 52, 54, 83
North Beach, 75
Nyad, Diana, 99

Old Rhodes Key, 16, 19
Old Seven Mile Bridge, 50, 92, 94
Osceola, 9
Overseas Highway, 12–13, 15, 36, 44, 50, 60
Overseas Railroad, 11–12, 18, 37, 38, 49, 93

Pennekamp, John, 27
Pigeon Key, 50–51, 92
Plantation Key, 34, 36
Ponce de León, Juan, 7, 70

Quinn, Laura, 32

Ragged Keys, 16

San Pedro Underwater Archaeological Preserve State Park, 42
Sand Key, 11
Sands Key, 16
Sandspur Beach, 54
Seminole Nation, 8–9
Seven Mile Bridge, 13, 44, 52
shipwrecks, 9–11, 14, 18, 20, 21–23, 30, 32, 37, 40–41, 42, 59, 66–67, 76, 97–98
Smathers Beach, 99
Sombrero Beach, 46, 92, 97
South Beach, 75
Southernmost Point Buoy, 72
Sugarloaf Key, 52

Tequesta nation, 6–7
Totten Key, 16, 19
Truman, Harry S., 63

Upper Matecumbe Key, 34, 37–39

Virginia Key, 6

Williams, Tennessee, 63
Windley Key, 34, 36–37
wrecking, 9–10, 18, 40–41, 92–93

Yamasee Nation, 8
Yuchi nation, 8

ABOUT THE AUTHOR

PAM BERKMAN

Pam Berkman has written books for adults and kids. She visited the Florida Keys many years ago and has always remembered the Overseas Highway as the most magical road she has ever been on.